GOOD GOVERNANCE:

Issues, Signs and Solutions
[ISaS]

Jonathan Oyibo PMP

ISBN: 9798339412410

DEDICATION

I dedicate this book to Her and the
Hopefuls!
To My Late Wife, Rita;
To My Country, Nigeria;
To All Nations For Good Governance; and
To All Students Of Good Governance.

CONTENTS Page

FOREWARD

ON this day, the third day of August in the year twenty-twenty-four (*year two thousand and twenty-four*), I was relaxing at home in remembrance of the sixth anniversary of my beloved late wife, Rita, while the *#EndBadGovernance...* protest was in its third day in Nigeria. It was at this point I got inspired to put all the points I have often considered and compiled overtime on good governance into a book form for easy reading. And I think it will make some sense for leaders and followers, teachers and students in society and schools to get some learning from these simple ideas about good governance.

This Book, **GOOD GOVERNANCE: Issues, Signs and Solutions**, exposes some of the mistakes, and the consequences thereof, that Leaders often make in the administration and governance of their societies. The book also proffers some solutions and corrective actions that may help out if well applied. It, therefore, makes an excellent attempt to respond positively to ending bad governance, in order to foster good governance for an egalitarian society.

As a positive optimist, I am always averse to negative protests. I will rather go for a positive protest like *#StartGoodGovernance...,*
#StartGoodGovernaceInAfrica, and
#StartGoodGovernanceInAllNations.
I believe that the tagline or title of an event whether it is a rally, protest or contest, always determines what is being inspired and promoted, and expected as the outcome as well. A positive tagline promotes and engenders a positive outcome and vice versa. Hence, I like to go for *#StartGoodGovernance...,* and not the other way round.

That is what I am doing right now in this book with a positive title of *Good Governance*, and most of the suggestions I have put across here may respond to *"how to start good governance and sustain it"* in a society where it is either lacking or requires improvement. I have identified some common *Issues* related to lack of good governance and some of the *Signs* that the citizens or stakeholders may experience. The *Issues and Signs* mentioned in this book are some of the *characteristics* of lack of good governance. Expectedly, I have also proffered some *Solutions* related to fostering and promoting good governance for an egalitarian society. Therefore, using an **"ISaS Model"** (the Issues, Signs and Solutions Model), this book attempts to cover the good governance system for a society, especially where the trust and confidence of the people, followers or citizens are willingly entrusted to a few leaders to govern the society.

Good Governance is the master key to the wellbeing, welfare and security of the citizens, the environment and the society.

Happy reading!

Jonathan Oyibo PMP

INTRODUCTION TO GOOD GOVERNANCE:
Issues, Signs and Solutions

What is Good Governance?

FOR the purpose of the book, I will refer to Governance as the manner and pattern applied to govern, rule, or control a society [*a Community, Local Government, State, County, Nation, Country or an Institution*], with respect to the management of her economic and social resources.

Therefore, Good Governance is the application of good manners and patterns to govern, rule, or control a society [*a Community, Local Government, State, County, Nation, Country or an Institution*], in line with the existing rule of law, in order to achieve the developmental goals and prosperity level [*living standards*] set for the society. In a project management perspective, Good Governance should involve setting the right strategic goals [Vision], developing robust strategic plans for the goals [Mission], and implementing the plans with a ruthless focus to achieve the goals [Excellent Execution]. The goals are the desired results which sum up to the vision which is the desired future state of the society imagined by the Leaders and feasibly agreeable to the people.

Thus, a Good Governance system should include identifying a desired future state of the society [vision], developing a strategy for arriving at that future state [mission], selecting the right leaders and supporting them with authority to deliver the right results that progressively enhance the standard of living of the people being governed, and the standard of the environment of the society, into the desired future state.

The Aims of Good Governance
Hence, the aims of Good Governance, among others, are:
1. To provide a good environment that progressively enhances the citizens' standard of living in the society.
2. To promote honesty, fairness and integrity in the governance on the society.
3. To promote justice for all in the society [both the majority and the minority] and to listen to the opinions, voices, and cries of all the people [including the majorities, minorities, specially-able and oppressed] in decision-making for the society.
4. To create a conducive culture that encourages the society and her officers to aim to achieve the best for the people [citizens] and the society at large.

5. To adherently promote the rule of law and significantly minimize corruption in the society.

The process of good governance must ensure that the public institutions conduct public affairs and manage the public resources in a manner and pattern that adheres to the rule of law, for the common good of the people and society.
In summary, therefore, good governance aims to minimize corruption, take into account the opinions of minorities, and listen to the voices of the oppressed people in decision-making for societal general good.

Good Governance can be a *"Walk in the Park,"* if the right principles and standards are set and followed in its practice. These principles, which has to be demonstrated both in word and action, include effective leadership and management, transparency, accountability, integrity, stewardship and the rule of law. The principle of the rule of law plays a pivotal role that provides the framework for decision-making, action and justice in the society.

As a crucial aspect of a functioning society, it is essential to understand the *Issues and Signs* affecting good governance and resulting from lack of *Good Governance*, and proffer some *Solutions* that promote and encourage the process effectively.

Good Governance is different from Good Government. Governance is a Process; while the Government is the Body of Leaders [the Executive, Legislature and Judiciary] put in place to rightly implement the governance process in trust. Therefore, with good governance, the processes and institution produce results that meet society's needs with the best use of the available resources.

Bad leaders cannot endure for long where there is a good governance template! The template can always discard, dismiss or throw out bad leadership very quickly. In this book, it is assumed that the Government [a group leaders or people in power] performs the function of governance in a society.

The Issues, Signs and Solutions [ISaS] Model

Here is a comprehensive overview of the Issues, Signs and Solutions [ISaS] Model for Good Governance:

The Issues

Some of the probable Issues that affect good governance are listed here:

1. Ineffective Leadership and Management - lack of a proper vision, ineffective public service and corruption.

2. Lack of Transparency and Accountability by the Leaders and Government
3. Over-centralization of power - abuse of power
4. Weak institutions
5. Inadequate citizen participation
6. Inequality and discrimination
7. Illicit enrichment and conflict of Interests
8. Inefficient complex manual processes
9. Limited civic education and awareness
10. Weak rule of law
11. Mismanagement of economic and natural resources, and resistance to reforms
12. Lack of collaborative leadership
13. Poor decision-making

The resultant outcome and loss arising from bad governance or lack of good governance is acute and severe social, economic, and political crisis and instability.

The Signs

Some of the probable Signs are listed here:
1. Poor economic performance - social and economic crises.
2. Lack of trust in government and lack of public confidence.
3. Inefficient public services, bad service delivery, bribery and corruption.
4. Lack of checks and balances, ineffective oversight mechanisms and corruption within institutions.

5. Lack of representation, disengagement from the political processes and political crisis.

6. Incompetence in public office - nepotism, cronyism and political polarization.

7. Illicit enrichment and widespread corruption among public officers and officials.

8. Inadequate access to information.

9. Lack of civic knowledge and vulnerability to misinformation.

10. Human rights abuses and violations - social unrest and protests.

11. Resistance to change.

12. Lack of coordination among agencies and inadequate stakeholder engagement.

13. Lack of data-driven decision-making and lack of evidence-based policy and program development.

These Signs, when unattended to, can lead to the failure of the governance in a society.

When Good Leaders are seen as Bad: My Nigeria's Anecdote

A one-time good and successful leader can misconstrued and become seen as a bad leader when he starts giving no attention to the hardship being experienced by the people, and giving deaf ears to the cries of the followers.

The same way, good governance often collapses into bad governance when the leaders in authority and trust fail to address the concerns of the citizens, the people and followers. The lack of good governance or collapse of it can lead to social and political crises and protests.

Such crises or protests may start quietly in an implicit zone, and then grow with a strong twist into the explicit zone, resulting in major crises and protests at full-blast, especially when the grievances of the people [citizens] are unattended to and the potential protests nipped in the bud when still in the quiet implicit zone. It is very important and expedient for the leaders of the society to quickly call the representatives of the aggrieved people or followers to listen to them and discuss all their grievances to avoid explicit protests.

In Nigeria, before the #EndBadGovernance protests started in the streets on the first of August in 2024, about one month's notice was claimed and presumed to have been given to the government by the perceived organizers [as seen in some social media, though not clearly identified at the beginning], with a list of their grievances and requests, and reasons for the protests which included the increasingly deteriorating economy, hardship and hunger being experienced by the mass of people in the country, while the leaders of the country were seemingly not affected and concerned about these economic vices, as perceived by the people.

As a rough and sketchy account, the government tried to stop the protests by coercion, instead of calling for round table negotiations, and the ultimate Leadership of the country eventually addressed the nation directly some days after the protests had gone into its explicit zone; yet it was perceived by the protestants that none of their requests and concerns were not addressed in the address of the ultimate Leadership to the people and citizens of the country. The protests began to take a twist from #EndBadGovernance protests to a more serious protest against the ultimate leadership and government of the current regime. Destruction of properties then started to take the toll through perceived miscreants who might have infiltrated into some peaceful protest groups, and were now making direct attack at some government and political representatives, targeting their properties. These incidents were very outrageous!

Nevertheless, if the government is for the people, it is obligatory for the government to always listen to the people for good governance to prevail! This encourages citizen participation.

The Solutions

Some key strategies for promoting good governance are listed here.

1. Set clear vision, goals and objectives – for the citizens' and environment's well-being, welfare and security.

2. Promote transparency and accountability – to gain public trust.

3. Encourage citizen participation – to build citizen and public trust

4. Strengthen institutions – for unbiased decisions.

5. Implement anti-corruption measures – asset and interests declarations, etc

7. Implement a merit –based appointment system – to address inequality and discrimination.

8. Simplify and digitalize the processes – to easy access to informal and avoid complex manual processes.

9. Education and awareness – to improve the public services and citizens' awareness through capacity building training, smart goals setting, national orientation.

10. Effective Rule of Law – to support good governance practices

11. Implement gradual reforms – to foster economic and political stability and development.

12. Implement collaborative leadership approach and cross-functional dialogue.
13. Continuous monitoring and evaluation of the performance of the System – to effective measure and evaluate performance, make adjustments and corrective actions and make informed decisions.

By understanding these issues, signs, and solutions, we can work towards promoting good governance and creating a more just, equitable, and prosperous society.

ONE

EFFECTIVE LEADERSHIP AND MANAGEMENT

What are Effective Leadership and Management?

EFFECTIVE Leadership and Management in society refer to the ability of individuals or groups to guide, direct and administer resources to achieve a common vision, goals and objectives for the society.

Effective Leadership

Specifically, Effective Leadership is the ability to inspire, motivate and empower others [most often followers] to work towards a common vision or goal. It involves, among others, features:

o Brilliant Communication of a clear vision and expectations.

o Strategic thinking to develop plans to achieve set goals.

o Emotional intelligence to manage one's emotions and those of others.

- Empowerment by delegating authority and encouraging ownership of responsibilities.
- Accountability by taking responsibility for actions and outcomes.
- Integrity by demonstrating ethics, values and transparency.
- Collaboration to build and maintain effective relationships.

Effective Management

Specifically, Effective Management refers to achieving desired results by getting things done through people. It involves planning, organizing, leading, and controlling of resources to achieve specific goals and objectives, through some other detailed activities like:

- Clear goal-setting by establishing measurable and achievable objectives.
- Efficient and effective allocation of resources
- Prioritization to focus on high-impact activities and tasks
- Risk management to identify and mitigate potential risks.
- Performance monitoring to track progress and adjust strategies.

o Problem-solving to address challenges and find solutions.
o Accountability to take responsibility for outcomes and results.

In every setting including governance, effective leadership and management begin with a clear vision, and clear goals and objectives. This means defining the desired future state of the society, deciding on the deliverables, milestones and metrics, and sharing them with the stakeholders including the citizens of the society. A good understanding of the objectives and outcomes should be ensured. Everyone is expected to know and understand them. It also means ensuring that stakeholders understand the governance purpose and outcomes. This clarity enables both the Leaders [government in power] and the people [citizens] to be aligned in good governance without much friction.

A. The Issues: *What are the core Issues in Effective Leadership and Management?*

Ineffective Leadership and Management is the issue here.

The Issues of ineffective leadership and management in a society cover the following areas:

o Lack of clear vision and direction, which means that there are no clear vision, goals and objectives for the Leaders to focus on and share with the citizens.

o Inadequate planning and prioritization

o Inefficient resources allocation and management.

o Poor talent management and succession planning.

o Ineffective conflict resolution and crisis management.

o Poor Collaborative Leadership. [*This is addressed in more details in chapter twelve.*]

B. The Signs: *What are the Signs of Ineffective Leadership and Management in Governance?*

Here are some major Signs to watch out for to know when the society lacks effective leadership and management in governance:

o Conflicting priorities.

o Poor communication of vision.

o Poor stakeholders' engagement.

o Poor service delivery and quality.

o Unclear policies - poor policy decisions and outcomes.
o Low morale, high turnover rates and brain drain.
o Governance and leadership crises.

C. The Solutions: *The Implications! What Solutions can help?*

Provide and enforce effective Leadership and Management, setting and communicating a clear vision and direction for the society.

The Purpose: The purpose of effective leadership and management is to set and communicate a clear vision, smart goals and objectives for the citizens' and environment's well-being, welfare and security.

Here are some corrective solutions to address the issues and signs of ineffective leadership and management in governance.

1. *Define a clear vision and develop GAME plans for good governance:* The first thing to be done is to assess the current situation of the society, analyze the challenges and identify areas for improvement. These Leadership and Management actions will then define, develop and provide clear vision and direction for good governance in the society, and establish or set

clear and relevant goals and objectives to focus on. *GAME Plans here mean the Goals, Activities, Measurement and Evaluation Plans.* The GAME Plans contain the goals and activities to pursue and implement, and the measurement and evaluation plans for the results of governance. In summary, this solution requires establishing clear goals and objectives; setting priorities through stakeholders' engagement; aligning resources with the priorities; and regularly reviewing and adjusting the priorities.

2. *Effectively communicate the vision and GAME plan:* Share and communicate the Vision, Goals and Objectives with the citizens and stakeholders of the society, right from the start of the regime. In summary, this solution requires developing a communication strategy; engaging stakeholders through regular meetings and feedback mechanisms; and using multiple communication channels.

3. *Improve the delivery and quality of public services to engender citizens' satisfaction:* Conduct citizens' satisfaction surveys to identify areas for service improvement and develop service delivery standards and implement quality control measures.

4. *Establish evidence-based policy development and review processes:* Regularly review, update and clarify policies; engage stakeholders in policy development; communicate policies clearly to

stakeholders and regularly evaluate policy outcomes.

5. *Improve citizen morale and reduce turnover rates and brain drain:* To conduct stakeholders' engagement surveys to undercover and address underlying issues and concerns; and to develop retention strategies and foster a positive work culture through training and development opportunities.

6. *Conduct governance and leadership assessments, and development plans:-* Establish clear roles and responsibilities to foster a culture of responsibility and accountability

7. *Collaborative Leadership and Partnership:* Foster a collaborative and inclusive approach to decision-making.

These corrective solutions can help address the signs of ineffective leadership and management in governance, leading to improved governance, service delivery, and stakeholders' satisfaction.

Examples of Effective Leadership and Management in Some Countries

Here are some examples of societies that operate efficient leadership and management in governance:

1. Singapore's Corruption-Free Governance:
Singapore's leadership has implemented strict anti-corruption measures, making it one of the least corrupt countries globally.
2. *Finland's Education System:* Finland's education leadership has prioritized equity, inclusivity, and teacher training, resulting in one of the world's top-performing education systems.
3. *New Zealand's Response to COVID-19:* New Zealand's government demonstrated effective crisis management, swift decision-making and transparent communication, resulting in one of the world's best responses to the pandemic.
4. *Denmark's Green Transition:* Denmark's leadership has set ambitious climate goals, invested in renewable energy, and implemented sustainable policies, making it a global leader in green transition.
5. *Canada's Inclusive Immigration Policy:* Canada's government has implemented an inclusive immigration policy, welcoming diversity, and providing support for newcomers, resulting in a highly successful integration model.
6. *Sweden's Digital Governance:* Sweden's leadership has invested in digital infrastructure, made government services accessible online, and prioritized digital inclusion, making it a global leader in digital governance.

7. *Costa Rica's Environmental Conservation:* Costa Rica's government has prioritized environmental protection, invested in reforestation, and promoted eco-tourism, resulting in a significant increase in biodiversity and environmental sustainability.

8. *Estonia's E-Governance:* Estonia's leadership has implemented a comprehensive e-governance system, making most government services available online, and promoting digital citizenship.

9. *The audacious launch of the Dangote Refinery in Nigeria:* In Nigeria, there is an opportunity area in the petroleum industry where only one private firm *[the Dangote Refinery]* has audaciously demonstrated a daring level of effective leadership and management recently, by swimming against the turbulent current to launch a private mega refinery and started selling gasoline in Nigeria in October 2024, after the country had continuously imported gasoline for over a quarter of a century [over 25 years]. This is a very excellent example of effective leadership and management audacity by the *Dangote organization* in Nigeria. It is brilliantly an award-winning feat! The people of Nigeria and the Region definitely look forward with hope to experiencing the benefits of the refinery in that area, and to see more organizations taking a cue from the impressive example of this *leadership and management dexterity.*

These examples demonstrate efficient leadership and management in governance, resulting in positive outcomes for citizens and societies.

TWO

TRANSPARENCY AND ACCOUNTABILITY

What are Transparency and Accountability?

TRANSPARENCY And Accountability [T&A] are essential components of good governance. Transparency refers to the openness and clarity of government decision-making processes, policies, and actions. Accountability refers to the responsibility of government officials to answer for their actions and decisions. Lack of these essential components in governance can be a major issue for serious attention. For a good governance system to exist in a society, 'T&A' must apply!

A. The Issue - *What are the core Issues in Transparency and Accountability?*

Corruptions and Lack of Transparency and Accountability in implementing the affairs of governance are core issues.

B. The Signs: *What are the Signs of lack of Transparency and Accountability in governance?*

Major Signs that may manifest from the Issues of lack of Transparency and Accountability include the following:
o Widespread and endemic corruption.
o Inefficient use of public resources and budget overruns.
o Lack of trust and credibility among stakeholders, and loss of confidence in the government and leaders by the citizens.
o Unaccountable decision-making that lacks guidelines and transparency.

C. The Solutions: *The Implications! What solutions can help?*

Promote and implement Transparency and Accountability in society.

The Purpose: The purpose of Transparency and Accountability in governance is to gain and sustain the trust of the citizens and the people of the society.

Here are some corrective solutions to address the issues and signs of corruption and lack of transparency and accountability in governance:

1. *Implement anti-corruption programs*: To promote and foster a culture of transparency and accountability.
2. *Efficient use of resources and strict budget implementation:* Conduct resource allocation analysis and implement budgeting and financial management systems; prioritize resource allocation and regularly monitor and review resource use.
3. *Build trust and credibility among stakeholders:* Foster transparency and accountability; engage stakeholders in decision-making; communicate effectively and regularly and address concerns and issues promptly.
4. *Implement open-governance systems:* To ensure that citizens can access information and track government activities.

   Implementing transparency and accountability through open governance systems may involve and include several key components that can address complex challenges of good governance, such as:

   1) Freedom of Information Act: Enact legislation ensuring citizens' right to access government information and data.

2) Open Data Initiatives: Publish government vision, goals, objectives, key performance indicators, key results area, data, budgets, and expenditures in easily accessible formats.

3) Regular Audits and Reports: Conduct regular audits and publish reports on government activities, finances, and performance against goals. To measure and evaluate government performances periodically - monthly, quarterly, semi-annually and annually.

4) Citizen Engagement Platforms: Establish online and offline platforms for citizens to provide feedback, suggestions, and complaints.

5) Whistleblower Protection: Enact laws that encourage whistleblowers and protect them from retaliation and ensure their safety.

6) Independent Media and Press Freedom: Foster a free and independent press to hold government accountable.

7) Public Declarations of Assets: Mandate public declarations of assets by politicians and public officials.

8) Open Contracting and Procurement: Make government contracts and procurement processes transparent and accessible.

9) Citizen Participation in Goals Setting and Budgeting: Involve citizens in setting the common goals and budgeting processes through participatory planning and budgeting initiatives.

10) Citizen Participation in Goals Setting and Budgeting: Involve citizens in setting the common goals and budgeting processes through participatory planning and budgeting initiatives.

11) Digitalization and Technology: Leverage technology to enhance transparency, accountability, and citizen engagement.

By implementing these measures, open governance systems can help address challenges like corruption and mismanagement of public resources. This will ultimately promote good governance through transparency and accountability in the society.

It is also worthwhile to mention some of the key principles and benefits of Transparency and Accountability in governance, along with the mechanisms for activating them.

Some Key Principles of Transparency:

1. *Clear Information:* Government information is accurate, complete, and easily accessible.
2. *Open Decision-Making:* Decision-making processes are transparent, inclusive, and participatory.
3. *Public engagement:* Citizens are involved in policy-making and decision-making processes.
4. *Disclosure of interests:* Government officials disclose their interests and assets.

Some Key Principles of Accountability:

1. *Responsibility:* Government officials are responsible for their actions and decisions.
2. *Answerability:* Officials answer to citizens, parliament, and other oversight bodies.
3. *Enforceability:* Mechanisms exist to enforce accountability, such as sanctions and penalties.
4. *Performance monitoring:* Government performance is regularly monitored and evaluated.

Some Key Benefits of Transparency and Accountability:

1. *Trust and credibility:* Citizens trust government decisions and actions.

2. *Prevention of corruption:* Transparency and accountability reduce corruption and abuse of power.

3. *Improved decision-making:* Informed decision-making leads to better policies and outcomes.

4. *Citizen participation:* Transparency and accountability encourage citizens' engagement and participation.

5. *Good governance:* Transparency and accountability promote good governance and democratic values.

Some Mechanisms for Transparency and Accountability:

1. Freedom of Information Acts.
2. Whistleblower protection.
3. Independent oversight bodies.
4. Audits and evaluations.
5. Public reporting and disclosure.
6. Citizen engagement and participation mechanisms.
7. Anti-corruption agencies.
8. Parliamentary oversight.

By implementing these principles, mechanisms and ensuring the benefits realization, governments can ensure transparency and accountability, leading to good governance and the promotion of democratic values.

Some Examples of Transparency and Accountability in Action

Here are some examples of Transparency and Accountability in governance of some societies:

a. Transparency:
1. Open Budget Initiatives: Governments publish detailed budget information, like Open Budget Index (OBI) in the United States.

2. Freedom of Information Acts: Laws granting citizens access to government information, like the Freedom of Information Act (FOIA) in the United States and Nigeria.

3. Public Declarations of Assets: Officials publicly declare their assets, like in the Philippines' Statement of Assets, Liabilities, and Net Worth [SALN]; Nigeria's Code of Conduct Bureau [CCB] Office handles assets declarations for public officers in Nigeria.

4. Open Data Initiatives: Governments may release data in easily accessible formats with links. Open Data provides citizen access to data about public services for ease of government performance evaluation and collaboration.

5. Citizen Engagement Platforms: Online platforms for citizens to participate in decision-making, like the Estonian e-Participation Portal.

b. Accountability:

1. Independent Anti-Corruption Agencies: These are Bodies that investigate and prosecute corruption crimes, like the Independent Corrupt Practices Commission [ICPC] and Economic and Financial Crimes Commission [EFCC] in Nigeria.

2. Auditor-Generals' Offices: Independent auditors reviewing government finances like the Auditor-General of Canada.

3. Ombudsman Offices: Independent investigators addressing citizen complaints like the Swedish Parliamentary Ombudsman. This is a Public Advocate Office.

4. Whistleblower Protection Laws: Laws safeguarding whistleblowers from retaliation, like the Whistleblower Protection Act in the United States.

5. Citizen Oversight Committees: Community-led committees monitoring government activities like the Citizen Oversight Committee in Kenya.

These examples illustrate how the mechanisms of transparency and accountability can promote open governance, citizen participation, and trust in government.

To promote transparency and accountability effectively, government agencies that are involved must operate without prejudice, must be seen to be unbiased, and must apply the rule of law without emotional bias, with the common good of the individual citizen and society in mind at all times.

THREE

DECENTRALIZATION AND DEVOLUTION OF POWER

What are Decentralization and Devolution?

DECENTRALIZATION And Devolution involve transferring power, resources, and decision-making authority from the central authority or central government to local levels or local governments. Both are related concepts in good governance with the same aim.

Decentralization
o   Specifically, Decentralization involves transferring decision-making authority and resources from central government to local governments or agencies.
o   It aims to improve efficiency, responsiveness, and accountability in service delivery.
o   It can be administrative [de-concentration] or political [devolution].

Devolution
o   Specifically, Devolution involves transferring *significant* decision-making authority and

resources to local governments or communities.
o Its aims at empowering local authorities to make decisions on matters affecting their jurisdictions.
o It often involves constitutional or legal changes to ensure autonomy and accountability.

A. The Issue: *What are the Issues in Decentralization and Devolution?*

Over-centralization of power and lack of local autonomy in governance are the core issues here. In these core Issues that affect good governance badly, power and authority are concentrated and limited to the central government, without adequate local autonomy in decision-making. This has given rise to lack of fiscal federalism, abuse of power, ineffective centralization of decision-making, confused application of unitary principles in a federalism, and acute adverse affect on good governance.

B. The Signs: *What are the major Signs for Over-centralization of power and lack of local autonomy in governance?*

Here are some major Signs that may manifest for over-centralization of power and lack of local autonomy in governance:
o Over-centralization of decision-making.

o Inequitable allocation and distribution of resources.
o Lack of fiscal federalism.
o Abuse of power.
o Inefficient service delivery.
o Disconnection between central government and local communities.
o Stunted development.

These Signs indicate the presence of underlying Issues, and they help to identify areas for improvement.

The Solutions: *The Implications! What Solutions can help?*

Decentralize and Devolve Power from Central Government to Local Authorities.
These actions call for empowering local governments to make decisions and manage resources, promoting fiscal federalism and unlocking growth and development rate at their pace accordingly.

By decentralizing power and resources, and empowering local authorities or local governments, the government can address the Issues and Signs seen as challenges in the area of over-concentration of power and lack of local autonomy.

The Purpose - The purpose of decentralization and devolution is to get government closer to the citizens, prevent abuse of power, and make quicker and more efficient decisions for effective implementation and governance.

In general, decentralization and devolution of power and authority can help to address challenges of good governance through the following actions:

1. *Constitutional Reforms:* Amend the constitution to establish clear parameters for decentralization and devolution.

2. *Local Government Autonomy:* Grant local governments' independence in decision-making, budgeting, and resource management.

3. *Transparent Resource Allocation:* Ensure transparent and equitable allocation of resources to local governments.

4. *Fiscal Federalism:* Allocate resources and revenues to local governments, enabling them to address local needs.

5. *Devolution of Powers:* Transfer or delegate specific powers and responsibilities to local governments, such as education, healthcare, and infrastructure.

6. *Capacity Building:* Train and equip local government officials to manage resources and make informed decisions.

7. *Citizen Participation:* Encourage citizen engagement in local decision-making processes through town hall meetings and public consultations.

8. *Accountability Mechanisms:* Establish accountability mechanisms to monitor local government performance and resource management.

9. *Phased Devolution:* Gradually devolve powers and responsibilities to local governments, allowing for adaptation and capacity building.

10. *Inclusive and Representative Local Governance:* Ensure local governments represent diverse interests and perspectives.

Some Benefits of Decentralization and Devolution

1. *Improved Service Delivery:* Local authorities better understand local needs.

2. *Increased Accountability:* Decision-makers are closer to citizens.

3. *Enhanced Citizen Participation:* Local communities can engage more effectively.

4. *More Efficient Allocation of Resources:* Local authorities can prioritize needs.

5. *It Promotes Democracy and Inclusivity:* Empowers marginalized communities.

Some Major Considerations:

Some of the major factors to consider for decentralization and devolution of power include the following areas:
1. *Capacity Building:* Local authorities may need training and resources.
2. *Funding:* Adequate funding must be ensured for local authorities.
3. *Coordination:* Central and local authorities must coordinate effectively.
4. *Accountability:* Mechanisms must be established to ensure accountability.

In summary, decentralization and devolution are essential in good governance as they promote local autonomy, accountability, and effective service delivery, leading to more inclusive and responsive governance. Decentralization and devolution can foster more responsive, accountable, and effective governance, ultimately promoting development and addressing complex challenges in society.

Some Examples of Decentralization and Devolution of Power

Here are some examples of Decentralization and Devolution:

a. Decentralization

1. *Brazil's Municipalization:* Transferred power and resources from the federal government to municipalities for healthcare, education, and infrastructure management.

2. *Indonesia's Regional Autonomy:* Granted provinces and districts greater autonomy to manage their own affairs, including healthcare, education, and infrastructure.

3. *South Africa's Local Government Reform:* Strengthened local governments' roles in service delivery, planning, and development.

b. Devolution:

1. *United Kingdom's Devolution to Scotland and Wales:* Transferred powers from the UK Parliament to the Scottish Parliament and Welsh Assembly, including healthcare, education, and agriculture.

2. *Spain's Autonomous Communities:* Granted regions like Catalonia, Basque Country, and Galicia significant autonomy in areas like healthcare, education, and taxation.

3. *Kenya's County Governments:* Established county governments with powers to manage healthcare, agriculture, and infrastructure, among others.

4. *Local Government Autonomy in Nigeria:* The supreme court of Nigeria gave a verdict that gave local government financial autonomy in 2024.

They can now make decisions and take actions without the usual approvals from the State Governments. This action will encourage good governance and discourage bad governance in the country, if well implemented.

c. Fiscal Decentralization
1. *Germany's Municipal Finance Reform:* These reforms increased municipalities' financial autonomy, allowing them to manage their own budgets and revenues.
2. *Australia's Local Government Financial Assistance Grants:* These grants provided funding to local governments for infrastructure and service delivery.
3. *Canada's Gas Tax Fund:* This transferred funds to municipalities for infrastructure development and maintenance.

These examples demonstrate how decentralization and devolution can empower local governments, promote regional development, and improve service delivery.

FOUR

INDEPENDENT INSTITUTIONS

What are Independent Institutions?

INDEPENDENT Institutions are bodies that operate separately from the government and other entities, providing checks and balances to ensure good governance. They also cover a body of Oversight Institutions and as part of regulatory agencies that play an important role in the governance system of a society. Such institutions include anti-corruption agencies, electoral agencies, human right commissions and the public complaints commission or ombudsman, and more.

A. **The Issue** - *What are the core Issues in Independent Institutions?*

Weak Government Institutions and Lack of Effective Oversight Mechanisms are core issues of governance.

These core issues involve:
o   Lack of autonomy and independence of government institutions.

- o Lack of checks and balances on government activities and operations.
- o Corruption within the Institutions

B. The Signs - *What are the major Signs of Weak Institutions and Oversight Bodies?*

Here are some major Signs that may manifest from the Issues of Weak Institutions and Ineffective Oversight mechanisms:

- o Ineffective oversight over government institutions and operations.
- o Political interference in institutional decision-making.
- o Failure to hold leaders accountable.
- o Corruption in institutions.
- o Electoral fraud – including electoral improprieties and votes appropriation.
- o Weak rule of law – including unfair discrimination in its applications and refusal to apply the law against offenders and sacred cows in government or the ruling party.
- o Inefficient governance – including inappropriate gravy trains and misappropriation of funds.

C. The Solutions: *The Implications - What Solutions can help?*

Build and Strengthen Independent Institutions and Oversight Bodies.

Strengthening the Independent Institutions and Oversight Bodies like Anti-corruption agencies, Electoral commissions, Human rights commission, the Judiciaries, and more can help to address the identified challenges and signs of week institutions in societies.

The Purpose - The purpose of building and strengthening Independent Institutions and Oversight Bodies is to provide checks and balances in governance and prevent abuse of power and political interference in institutional decision-making, and to hold leaders accountable.

Strengthening independent institutions and oversight bodies involves the following mechanisms and actions:

1. *Legislative Framework:* Establish or amend laws to ensure independence, autonomy, and clear mandates for these institutions.
2. *Appointment Processes:* Implement transparent, merit-based appointment processes for heads and members of these institutions.

3. *Security of Tenure:* Ensure security of tenure for the institutions' heads and members to prevent political interference.

4. *Adequate Funding:* Provide sufficient funding and resources to enable these institutions to function effectively.

5. *Clear Mandates:* Define clear, specific mandates for each institution to avoid overlap or confusion.

6. *Accountability Mechanisms:* Establish internal and external accountability mechanisms to monitor the institutions' performance.

7. *Capacity Building:* Provide training and capacity-building programs for the institutions' staff to enhance skills and expertise.

8. *Public Engagement:* Foster public trust and engagement through transparency, outreach, and education.

9. *Judicial Independence:* Ensure judicial independence through secure tenure, adequate funding, and clear mandates.

10. *Inter-Institutional Coordination:* Promote collaboration and coordination among independent institutions to address complex challenges.

Independent institutions and oversight bodies provide checks and balances, promote accountability, and ultimately ensure good governance, contributing to a more just and equitable society.

Some Examples of Independent Institutions and Oversight Bodies

Here are some examples of independent institutions and oversight bodies and their roles:

1. Anti-Corruption Agencies:
o They Investigate and prosecute corruption cases. E.g., the Nigeria's Independent Corrupt Practices Commission [ICPC], and Economic and Financial Crimes Commission [EFCC].
o They also Monitor government activities and report on corruption. E.g., the Kenya's Ethics and Anti-Corruption Commission.

2. Electoral Commissions:
o They Oversee electoral processes and ensure fairness. E.g., the Nigeria's Independent National Electoral Commission [INEC], and the Independent State Electoral Commission [ISEC]; and the South Africa's Independent Electoral Commission [IEC].
o They also Register voters, conduct elections, and announce results. E.g. the Ghana's Electoral Commission (GEC); INEC, and IEC.

3. *Judiciaries:*
o They interpret laws and ensure justice. E.g., the India's Supreme Court and the Nigeria's Supreme Court.
o They also provide checks and balances on Executive and Legislative powers. E.g., the United States' Supreme Court.

4. *Central Banks:*
o They regulate monetary policy and maintain economic stability. E.g., the Central Bank of Nigeria [CBN] and the European Central Bank [ECB]
o They also supervise and regulate financial institutions. E.g., Bank of England [BoE].

5. *Human Rights Commissions:*
o They Investigate human rights abuses and violations, and provide remedies. E.g., South Africa's Human Rights Commission.
o They promote human rights education and awareness. E.g., Canada's Human Rights Commission.

6. Auditor-General's Offices:

- They conduct audits of government finances and activities. E.g., the Nigeria's Auditor-General and the Australia's Auditor-General.
- They also report on government performance and accountability. E.g., the United Kingdom's National Audit Office.

These institutions play crucial roles in promoting the rule of law, accountability and good governance.

FIVE

CITIZEN PARTICIPATION

What is Citizen Participation?

CITIZEN Participation involves empowering citizens to contribute to decision-making processes, ensuring that their voices are heard and valued. In this way, the citizens have the opportunity to influence public decisions.

A. The Issue: *What are the core Issues in Citizen Participation?*

Limited Citizen Participation is a core issue.

This involves:
- Citizens' disengagement from the political processes.
- Lack of representation in the political process.
- Inadequate feedback mechanisms.

B. The Signs: *What are the major Signs for lack of Citizen Participation?*

Here are some major Signs to watch out for to know when there is lack of citizen participation in governance:
- o Feeling of disconnection from government.
- o Disregard for citizen feedback and concerns.
- o Limited access to information and decision-making processes.
- o Low voter turnout and engagement.
- o Unresponsive governance.

C. The Solutions: *The Implications - What Solutions can help?*

Develop and deploy Citizens Participation Programs, to encourage their engagement, representation and feedbacks in the governance process.

The Purpose - The purpose of Citizen Participation is to ensure that Citizens' voices are heard and valued, by encouraging and fostering citizens' engagement, adequate representation and feedback mechanisms in the political processes, and ultimately promoting responsive governance.

Here are some Citizen Participation programs and mechanisms to deploy to address complex challenges of bad governance facing a society:

1. *Inclusive Policy Making:* Involve citizens in policy development, implementation, and evaluation.

2. *Town Hall Meetings:* Organize regular town hall meetings for citizens to engage with government officials and discuss issues.

3. *Public Consultations:* Conduct public consultations on key policy issues, ensuring diverse perspectives are considered.

4. *Citizen Engagement Platforms:* Establish online and offline platforms for citizens to provide feedback, suggestions, and complaints.

5. *Representative Citizen Groups:* Establish representative groups to ensure diverse citizen voices are heard.

6. *Capacity Building:* Provide training and resources to citizens, enabling effective participation.

7. Feedback Mechanisms: Establish mechanisms to ensure citizen feedback is acknowledged and acted upon.

8. Transparency and Accountability (T&A): Ensure transparency in decision-making processes and accountability for actions taken. This has been treated in more details in chapter two of this book.

9. Inclusive Language: Use inclusive language and accessible formats to ensure all citizens can participate.

10. Continuous Evaluation: Regularly evaluate and improve citizen participation mechanisms.

By implementing these measures, citizen participation can help address complex challenges by:

o   Increasing trust in government
o   Fostering a sense of ownership and responsibility
o   Providing diverse perspectives and innovative solutions
o   Ensuring policies meet citizen needs
o   Promoting transparency and accountability
o   Strengthening democratic institutions

Therefore, effective citizen participation can also lead to more informed decision-making, better policy outcomes, a more engaged citizenry and good governance, ultimately contributing to a more resilient and prosperous Society.

Some Examples of Citizen Participation

Here are some examples of Citizen Participation programs and mechanisms:

1. *Participatory Budgeting:* Citizens contribute to budget decisions, like in Porto Alegre, Brazil.
2. *Town Hall Meetings:* Regular meetings between citizens and government officials like in Abuja, Nigeria, and in ancient Athens, Greece.

3. *Citizen Juries:* Randomly selected citizens deliberate on policy issues, like in the United States.

4. *Public Consultations:* Government solicits citizen input on policy proposals, like in Canada.

5. *Online Engagement Platforms:* Digital platforms for citizens to provide feedback and suggestions, like in Estonia.

6. *Citizen Engagement Committees:* Representative groups of citizens advising government, like in Australia.

7. *Co-Creation Initiatives:* Citizens collaborate with government to develop policies and services, like in Finland.

8. *Neighborhood Assemblies:* Local citizens gather to discuss and address community issues, like in Spain.

9. *Citizen-Led Advocacy Groups:* Grassroots organizations pushing for policy changes, like in the United States.

10. *National Citizen Engagement Strategies:* Comprehensive approaches to citizen participation, like in Scotland. In Nigeria, there is the National Orientation Agency [NOA] that was established in 1993 to re-orientate and encourage Nigerians to take part actively and freely in discussions and decisions affecting their general and collective welfare. The aim of the NOA is to foster national unity, patriotism and development by engaging citizens with

accurate and timely information about government policies, while gathering public opinion.

These examples demonstrate various ways citizens can contribute to decision-making processes, ensuring their voices are heard and valued in the administration and governance of the Society.

SIX

MERIT-BASED APPOINTMENTS

What is Merit-Based Appointment?

MERIT-BASED Appointment refers to the selection of individuals for positions or roles based on their merit, skills and qualification for the job. It ensures competence and that the most capable and qualified individuals are chosen for the job. It also reduces nepotism and cronyism in the public service.

A. The Issue: *What are the core Issues in Merit-Based Appointments?*

Lack of a Merit-Based Appointment System is a core issue.
A Federal Quota System [FQS] of appointment and unqualified individuals in key positions are major issues that affect good governance in a society.

B. The Signs: *What are the major Signs of Lack of Merit-Based Appointments System?*

Here are some major Signs to watch out for to know when there is a lack of merit-based appointments in a Society:

- ○ Incompetence in public office
- ○ Nepotism and cronyism in appointments
- ○ Lack of diversity in appointments
- ○ Political patronage
- ○ Inequality and Discrimination

C. The Solutions: *The Implications - What Solutions can help?*

Implement a merit-based appointment system to ensure competence in service. Appoint individuals based on qualification, skills, experience, performance and achievements. Stop considering political affiliations, personal connections, nepotism, favoritism and discrimination is appointing individuals to public offices.

The Purpose - The purpose of a merit-based appointment system is to replace a federal quota system with merit-based appointment system in order to prevent and avoid nepotism, cronyism, incompetence in public offices, lack of diversity in appointments and political patronage, among others.

Implementing merit-based appointments involves:

1. *Clear Job Descriptions:* Establishing specific requirements and qualifications for each position. Job requirements are clearly defined.
2. *Transparent Selection Processes:* Advertising vacancies, using independent panels, and evaluating candidates based on merit and well established selection criteria.
3. *Competency-Based Assessments:* Using tests, interviews, and evaluations to assess candidates' skills and abilities. A competitive process of assessment and selection
4. *Independent Appointment Committees:* Establishing committees to oversee the selection process and ensure impartiality.
5. Diverse Candidate Pools: Encouraging applications from a broad range of candidates to ensure diversity.
6. Performance-Based Evaluations: Regularly evaluating appointees' performance to ensure they meet expectations. Decisions are based on evidence and objective evaluation.

Some Benefits of a Merit-Based Appointment System

By implementing a merit-based appointment system, the society can:
1. Reduce nepotism and cronyism.

2. Increase competence and effectiveness.
3. Enhance transparency and accountability.
4. Foster a culture of meritocracy.
5. Attract top talent to government and public institutions.
6. Improve public trust and confidence in government.

Some Examples of a Merit-based Appointment System

1. *Civil Service Exams:* Competitive examinations for government positions, like in Nigeria and the United States.
2. *Independent Judicial Appointments:* Merit-based selection of Judges, like in the United Kingdom.
3. *Merit-Based University Admissions:* Selecting students based on academic achievement, like in Australia and Nigeria *[Nigeria has a Unified Tertiary Matriculation Examination - UTME by the Joint Admission Matriculation Board – JAMB]*
4. *Competitive Bidding for Government Contracts:* Awarding contracts to the most qualified and cost-effective bidders.
5. *Professional Certification Programs:* Requiring certifications or licenses for certain professions, like medicine or law.
6. *Transparent Promotion Processes:* Promoting employees based on performance and merit, like in the private sector.

A merit-based appointment approach can help address the complex challenges of governance by ensuring that the most qualified individuals are in positions to make informed decisions and drive positive change, leading to better outcome and good governance.

Good Governance

SEVEN

DECLARATION OF ASSETS AND INTERESTS

What is Declaration of Assets and Interests?

DECLARATION of Assets and Interests is a process of documentation whereby public officers, officials, leaders or employees are required to submit for disclosure their records of incomes, assets, liabilities, and interests.

Assets Declaration

This is a tool for public servants and officers to check illicit enrichment of public officers and manage any potential conflict of interests, thereby ultimately promoting public trust. It is used to record their income, assets and liabilities with the bureau.

Interests Declarations

This is a process whereby public officers officially state and make known their connections with interests that may influence their judgment, decision-making, and actions in public offices.

It means to disclose a public officer's prejudicial connection with an affair.

A. The Issue: *What are the core Issues of Declaration of Assets and Interests?*

There is Lack of effective declaration of assets and interests by public officers, officials and leaders, coupled with illicit enrichment and conflicts of interest.

B. The Signs: *What are the major Signs for lack of Asset Declarations?*

Here are some major Signs to watch out for to know when there is lack of effective declarations of assets and interests by public officers in a Society:
- Illicit enrichment and corruption among public officials.
- Inadequate Asset Declarations:
- Undeclared assets and conflicts of interest.
- Lack of transparency in financial dealings.
- Unexplained wealth and lavish spending.
- Failure to disclose assets and interests.

C. The Solutions: *The Implications -What Solutions can help?*

Enforce effective declarations of assets and interests of public officers.

The Purpose - The purpose of declaration of assets and interests is to prevent, detect, investigate and prosecute illicit enrichment, conflicts of interest, and corruption, and to promote transparency and build public trust among public officers or officials.

Mandating the declaration of assets and interests for politicians, public officers and officials involves:

1. *Legislation:* Enacting laws requiring asset declarations.
2. *Disclosure Forms:* Creating standardized forms for officials to report assets, liabilities, and interests.
3. *Verification Processes:* Establishing mechanisms to verify declared assets.
4. *Public Access:* Making declarations publicly available.
5. *Consequences for Non-Compliance:* Imposing penalties for false or incomplete declarations.

Some Benefits of Declarations of Assets and Interests

By implementing the declaration of assets and interest for public officers and officials, the

society can:
1. Reduce corruption
2. Increase transparency and accountability
3. Identify potential conflicts of interest
4. Build public trust
5. Deter illicit enrichment

Some Examples of Assets and Interests Declarations

Here are some examples of assets and interests declaration initiatives in some societies:
1. *United States' Financial Disclosure Forms:* Federal officials file annual forms disclosing financial interests.
2. *India's Lokpal Act:* Public officials declare assets, and the Lokpal investigates corruption complaints.
3. *South Africa's Public Service Regulations:* Officials declare financial interests to prevent conflicts of interest.
4. *Brazil's Transparency Portal:* Public officials' asset declarations are publicly accessible.
5. *Philippines' Statement of Assets, Liabilities, and Net Worth (SALN):* Public officials file annual SALNs, which are publicly available.
6. *The Nigeria's Code of Conduct Bureau (CCB):* This is a federal executive body set up by the Federal Government of Nigeria to establish and maintain high standards of public morality in the conduct of public businesses, ensuring conformity

of the behaviour of public officers with such high standards. They receive assets declarations by public officers.

Declaration of assets and interests can help address complex challenges of governance by promoting a culture of transparency and accountability among politicians and public officials.

EIGHT

SIMPLIFIED AND DIGITALIZED PROCESSES

What are simplified and digitalized processes?

SIMPLIFIED And Digitalized processes in a governance system refer to the application of non-complex procedures and use of automation and technology to perform tasks and transactions in the system.

Simplified Processes

These involve reduced bureaucracy, clear guidelines, efficient workflows and user-friendly interfaces in the system

Digitalized Processes

These involves use of technology, online platforms, electronic transactions, and digital documentations

A. The Issue: *What are the core Issues in Simplified and Digitalized Processes?*

Lack of simplified processes in governance is a core, because the processes are complex and manual, leading to inefficient service delivery.

B. The Signs: *What are the major Signs for lack of simplified processes in governance?*

Here are some major signs to watch out for to know when the processes of governance are so complex, manual and inefficient:
o   Bureaucratic red tape and delays
o   Lack of access to information and services
o   Inefficient use of resources
o   Corruption in manual processes
o   Frustration and dissatisfaction among citizens

C. The Solutions: *The Implications -What Solutions can help?*

Simplify and digitalize governance processes.

The Purpose: To make information and services more easily accessible to remove bureaucratic red tapes, to prevent inefficient use of resources, and to eradicate corruption in a manual process.

Simplifying and digitalizing governance processes involves:

1. *Process Mapping:* Identifying and analyzing existing processes.

2. *Streamlining:* Eliminating unnecessary steps and reducing complexity.

3. *Digitalization:* Automating processes using technology.

4. *Online Portals:* Creating user-friendly online platforms for citizens to access services.

5. *Inter-Agency Integration:* Enabling data sharing and coordination among government agencies.

6. *Citizen Engagement:* Involving citizens in the design and testing of new processes.

Some Benefits of Simplifying and Digitalizing the Processes of Governance

By simplifying and digitalizing processes, government /leaders can:

1. Serve the citizens better and promote good governance.
2. Reduce bureaucracy and corruption.
3. Increase efficiency and productivity.
4. Enhance citizen engagement and satisfaction
5. Improve transparency and accountability
6. Foster a more innovative and competitive economy.

Some Examples of Simplified and Digitalized Processes

Examples of simplified and digitalized processes include:

1. *Estonia's Digital Government:* Online portals for citizens to access various government services.

2. *India's Digital India Initiative:* Simplified and digitalized processes for citizens to access services.

3. *South Korea's Government 3.0 Initiative:* Streamlined and digitalized processes for increased efficiency.

4. *United States' Portal:* Centralized online platform for citizens to access government services.

5. *Singapore's Smart Nation Initiative:* Leveraging technology to streamline processes and enhance citizen engagement.

6. *Lagos State Internal Revenue Agency (LIRA):* This is a simplified and digitalized Tax Administration System in a State in Nigeria.

The simplified and digitalized approach can help address complex challenges by making government services more accessible, efficient, and responsive to citizens' needs.

NINE

EDUCATION AND AWARENESS

What is Education and Awareness in governance?

EDUCATION And Awareness in a governance system involve a deliberate effort to promote civic education, emphasizing the importance of transparency, accountability, and good governance, and fostering awareness on national legacy events, history and lessons thereof.

A. The Issues: *What are the core Issue in Education and Awareness?*

Limited Education and Awareness are core issues. They lead to citizens' disengagement from the political process, and inadequate critical thinking skills.

B. The Signs: *What are the major Signs for lack of Education and Awareness?*

Here are some major Signs to watch out for to know when the society is predominantly ignorant, and lacks civic education and awareness in their

political environment:
o Lack of civic knowledge and engagement
o Disregard for democratic values and principles
o Limited critical thinking and media literacy
o Vulnerability to misinformation and disinformation
o Apathy and disconnection from governance.

C. The Solutions: *The Implications - What Solutions can help?*

Implement citizens' education, awareness and enlightenment programs

The Purpose: To equip the citizens with the right knowledge and skills necessary to participate in governance and demand positive change

Promoting Education and Awareness for good governance involves:

1. *An Inclusive Civic Education Curriculum:* Promote civic education by emphasizing and integrating good governance, transparency, and accountability into schools curricula.

2. *Public Awareness Campaigns:* Organizing campaigns to educate citizens about their rights and responsibilities.

3. *Community Engagement:* Engaging citizens in discussions and activities that promote good governance.

4. *Capacity Building:* Training government officials, civil society, and citizens on good governance promises and practices.

5. *Access to Information:* Ensuring citizens have access to information about government activities and decisions.

6. *Access to Education Loans and Grants:* Giving students' loan and grant assistance to students in need.

7. *Implementing National Orientation and Sensitization programs:* Creating awareness and enlightenment for national programs and activities in order to get the citizens and leaders properly aligned and involved, and to know and understand the citizens' code and the sustainable governance promise.

Some Benefits of Education and Awareness Programs

By implementing citizens' education and awareness, the society can:

1. Empower citizens to demand good governance.
2. Increase transparency and accountability.
3. Foster a culture of civic engagement.
4. Enhance government responsiveness.
5. Build a more informed and active citizenry.

Some Examples of Education and Awareness Programs

Examples of education and awareness initiatives include:

1. *The Nigeria's National Orientation Agency [NOA], And Mass Mobilization for Self Reliance, Social Justice and Economic Recovery [MAMSER]:* Help in educating Nigerian citizens and leaders about their rights, responsibilities, the political process, government policies and governance promises, and much more.

2. *Kenya's Citizenship Education Program:* Educating citizens on their rights and responsibilities.

3. *India's National Literacy Mission:* Empowering citizens through literacy and civic education.

4. *South Africa's Active Citizenship Program:* Encouraging citizens to participate in governance.

5. *Brazil's Transparency Portal:* Providing citizens with access to government information.

6. *United States' Civics Education Initiative:* Promoting civic education in schools.

7. *The Nigeria's Student Loan Program:* To Encourage more access to education funds for higher education in difficult financial times.

In summary, the Education and Awareness approach can help address complex challenges of governance by equipping citizens with the knowledge and skills necessary to participate in governance and demand positive change.

TEN

EFFECTIVE RULE OF LAW

What is Effective Rule of Law?

RULE of Law is a fundamental concept in governance, which ensures that society is governed by a set of clear, publicized, and stable laws, rather than arbitrary decisions or personal interests. These laws are deemed to be supreme and all citizens including the rulers, leaders or government are expected to be subjected to the laws, and also entitled to be protected by the laws. The concept attempts to protect the rights of the citizens from arbitrary abuse by the power of government.

Effective Rule of Law, therefore, refers to the ability of the existing Laws of a Society to rule over every action of the rulers, leaders and the government of a Society.

The laws should give direction to all their actions. No one is expected to be above the law where there is effective Rule of Law.

Effective Rule of Law is characterized by key principles some of which include the following:

1. Legitimacy: The laws are clear, publicized, and accepted by the Society.
2. Impartiality: The laws are applied equally to all, without bias or favoritism in form of nepotism or cronyism.
3. Accountability: The government and officials are accountable for their actions.
4. Transparency: The decision-making processes are open and accessible.
5. Independence: The Judiciary and other institutions operate independently.

A. The Issue: *What is the core Issue with Rule of Law?*

Weak Rule of Law is a core issue.

This is when the Laws are weak and unable to rule effectively. The Issue of ineffective and weak rule of law in a society covers the following areas and more:
o   Inadequate and ineffective justice system.
o   Some Citizens and Institutions are not accountable to the laws.
o   The Laws are not equally enforced and independently adjudicated.
o   The Laws are not consistent with international human rights and standards.

B. The Signs: *What are the major Signs of Ineffective Rule of Law?*

Here are some major Signs to watch out for to know when the Society lacks effective Rule of Law in governance:

o Human rights abuses - Frequent attacks on members of the legal professions and human rights defenders

o Increasing lack of accountability and transparency of government institutions

o Excessive government power and Inadequate access to justice

o Weak legal institutions and Political Interference with the Laws

o Corruption with impunity – proceeds from illegal economy find their ways into government institutions leading to acute corruption.

o Socio-economic inequality – corruption diverts public resources from public services, increases poverty and hampers sustainable development of the society.

o Increasing insecurity and crimes rates – This is also an indication of a weak rule of law in a society.

o Overriding Executive powers over the Legislature and the Judiciary – weak separation of powers, which allows the executive arm to dominate the other arms of government.

○ Improprieties and crimes of political and public officials and officers are treated with levity and impunity.

The consequences of these signs of ineffective rule of law can be very severe and far reaching. They do not only diminish citizens' and other stakeholders' trust in the institutions, but also discourage investment and hinder economic growth and development in the society.

C. The Solutions: *The Implications -What Solutions can help?*

- **Implement and enforce effective Rule of Law, by providing a framework that ensures that power is exercised in a fair, accountable, and transparent manner, promoting justice, stability, and prosperity.**
- **Implement draconian laws to punish improprieties and crimes of public and political officers, leaders, and leaders who hold public offices in trust.**
  Like the saying goes, "Caesar's wife must be above suspicion."

The Purpose: The purpose of implementing an effective Rule of Law is to provide a framework for fair exercise of power and hold everyone accountable to the law in society.

Rule of Law should provide a framework for governance, ensuring that the following actions and standards are always in place and adhered to in the society:

1. Clear and consistent laws.
2. Independent and impartial judiciary.
3. Effective checks and balances, with clear separation of powers
4. Protection of human rights and fundamental freedoms.
5. Access to justice and fair trial.
6. Transparency and accountability in government.
7. Strong institutions and separation of powers.
8. Protection of property rights and contracts.
9. Effective dispute resolution mechanisms.
10. Respect for international law and agreements.
11. Equality before the law
12. Deliver severe consequences for public and political officers' and officials' improprieties and crimes.

Some Benefits of Effective Rule of Law

Here are some benefits that effective rule of law offers to the Society:

1. Predictability and stability in the Society.
2. Trust in institutions and government.
3. Respect and safeguard for human rights and dignity.

4. Economic growth and development.
5. Reduced corruption and impunity.
6. Equality of all individuals before the law.
7. All Individuals have rights to fair and public trial
8. The government is accountable to the people

Some Indicators of Effective Rule of Law:

1. Low corruption perception index
2. High ranking in global governance indices
3. Strong judicial independence
4. Effective access to information laws
5. Low levels of human rights abuses
6. High levels of citizen trust in institutions
7. Effective anti-money laundering frameworks
8. Robust asset recovery mechanisms
9. Effective whistleblower protection
10. International recognition and cooperation.

Effective Rule of Law fosters a stable, just, and prosperous Society, where citizens' rights are protected and respected, and institutions serve the public interest.

It provides a framework for good governance, ensuring that power is exercised in a fair, accountable, and transparent manner, promoting justice, stability, and prosperity.

ELEVEN

GRADUAL REFORMS

What are Gradual Reforms?

GRADUAL Reforms refer to a series of gentle but incremental changes in some sequence in order to improve the efficiency, effectiveness, and accountability of institutions, policies, and processes for good governance in a society.

For gradual reforms to be effective and to enhance good governance, they should come with some characteristics as follows:

1. *Incremental:* The reforms should be delivered in small, manageable changes.

2. *Sequential:* Each reform should be implemented to build on previous reforms.

3. *Long-term focus:* The reforms should consider sustainability over quick fixes.

4. *Stakeholder engagement:* The reforms should involve an inclusive, participatory approach.

5. *Evidence-based:* The reforms should foster data driven decision-making.

6. *Flexibility:* The reforms should be adaptable to changing circumstances.

A. The Issues: *What are the core Issues that lead to Gradual Reforms?*

Several governance issues that lead to gradual reforms cut across multifaceted areas of government Institutions, Policies, Administrations, the Economy, and Socio-political challenges. The Issues are numerous and include the following and more:

- Weak and inadequate institutional capacity.
- Policy inconsistencies.
- Inefficient public service delivery.
- Lack of citizen-centric services.
- Inefficient economic regulation.
- Economic uncertainty.
- Political uncertainty and lack of political will.
- Inequality and social exclusion
- Human Rights violations
- Limited democracy and electoral irregularities

B. The Signs: *What are the major Signs that indicate that Reforms are needed?*

Here are some signs to indicate that reforms are required in a Society:

- Economic Instability.
- Political Instability.
- Lack of economic development and growth.
- Lack of trust in government and institutions.

Some Challenges To Reforms

Reforms always come with some challenges.
These challenges may include the following:

1. Resistance to reforms.

2. Fear of change and uncertainty.

3. Resistance to new ideas and perspectives.

4. Unintended consequences of reforms.

C. The Solutions: *The Implications - What Solutions can help?*

Implement Gradual Reforms across various sections of the public service and functions. These gradual reforms should cover institutional reforms, policy reforms, administrative reforms, economic reforms, legal reforms, social reforms and political reforms to foster good governance in the society.
These reforms have to be gradual in order to overcome the various challenges of implementing reforms.

The Purpose: The purpose of implementing Gradual Reforms is to improve the effectiveness and efficiency of governance in society.

Implementing gradual reforms involves:
1. *Phased Implementation:* Breaking down large-scale reforms into smaller, manageable phases.

2. *Pilot Programs:* Testing reforms on a small scale before scaling up.

3. *Incremental Changes:* Introducing small, incremental changes to existing systems.

4. *Stakeholder Engagement:* Engaging with stakeholders to build support and address concerns.

5. *Monitoring and Evaluation:* Continuously monitoring and evaluating reforms to inform adjustments.

Transformative change takes time, effort, and perseverance. By adopting an incremental approach, governments can build momentum, ensure sustainability, and create lasting impact.

Some Benefits of Gradual Reforms

By implementing gradual reforms, the Leaders, Government and Society can:

1. Minimize disruption and resistance.

2. Allow for adaptation and learning.

3. Build support and consensus from the citizens.

4. Test and refine the reforms.

5. Achieve sustainable long-term change.

6. Increase stability, economic grow and predictability.
7. Improve institutional capacity.
8. Enhance accountability and transparency.
9. Achieve better service delivery and citizen engagement
10. Reduce corruption and inequality

This approach can help address complex challenges by introducing reforms in a manageable, incremental manner, allowing for adaptation and minimizing resistance.

Some Types of Reforms:

1. *Institutional Reforms:* To strengthen or establish new institutions.
2. *Policy Reforms:* To improve policy frameworks and regulations.
3. *Administrative Reforms:* To enhance public administration and service delivery.
4. *Legal Reforms:* To update laws and judicial systems.
5. *Economic Reforms:* To promoting economic growth and stability.
6. *Other forms of reforms:* These may include political reforms, electoral reforms, educational reforms, etc.

Some International Organizations That Support Gradual Reforms:

1. World Bank's Governance and Institutional Development.
2. United Nations Development Program's (UNDP) Governance and Peace building.
3. European Union's (EU) Governance and Institutional Capacity Building.
4. Organization for Economic Co-operation and Development's (OECD) Public Governance Reviews.
5. International Monetary Fund's (IMF) Fiscal Governance and Institutional Capacity Building.

Some Examples of Gradual Reforms

1. *Civil Service Reforms:* Improving recruitment, training, and promotion processes.
2. *Budgetary Reforms:* Enhancing transparency, accountability, and fiscal discipline.
3. *Anti-Corruption Reforms:* Strengthening anti-corruption agencies and laws.
4. *Electoral Reforms:* Improving voting systems, campaign finance, and voter registration.
5. *Healthcare Reforms:* Incremental improvements in healthcare access, quality and financing.

Some Country Examples of Successful Gradual Reforms

1. *Singapore's Economic Reforms:* Singapore's gradual transformation into a modern, efficient state. The Country gradually introduced market-oriented reforms to transition from a state-led to a market-led economy.
2. *New Zealand's Public Sector Reforms:* Implementing incremental reforms to improve public sector efficiency and effectiveness.
3. *Sweden's Healthcare Reforms:* Gradually introducing market-based reforms to improve healthcare quality and access.
4. *Canada's Tax Reform:* Implementing phased tax reforms to simplify and reduce taxes.
5. *Australia's Education Reforms:* Introducing incremental changes to improve education quality and accessibility.
6. *Nigeria's National Economic Reforms:* The Government of Nigeria introduced the National Economic Empowerment and Development Strategy (NEEDS) in year 2003 to support the creation of wealth, generation of employment, and reduction of poverty in order to bring about development in the Country.
7. *Estonia's e-government and digitalization reforms:* This is a long-term reform strategy introduced in 1998 as a guiding principle to empower citizens through digital solutions.

8. South Africa's post-apartheid institutional reforms: These involved constitutional reforms after 1994 to completely abolish Apartheid, put democracy in place and give rights to the blacks to vote.

9. Brazil's anti-corruption and transparency reforms: These reforms that started with an Anti-corruption law enacted in 2013 introduced the Public Integrity System in Brazil, and the transparency, public participation and oversight on every stage of the life-cycle of big infrastructure projects in Brazil

10. India's gradual economic liberalization and governance reforms: These reforms refer to a series of policy changes aimed at opening up India' economy to the world through market-orientation and consumption-drive since 1991.

TWELVE

COLLABORATIVE LEADERSHIP

What is Collaborative Leadership?

COLLABORATIVE Leadership is a leadership style that inspires and involves cross-functional stakeholders to partake in fostering common societal goals. It is a leadership that emphasizes sharing power, decision-making, and responsibility among stakeholders to achieve common goals. It promotes an environment of mutual respect, trust, and open communication. With good collaborative leadership in governance, the various arms of government should not be working at cross roads. There should be unity of purpose among them, even including the opposition parties, since the welfare, betterment and common good of the Society is the ultimate goal of government. This is why collaborative leadership is called out for more attention in the effective Leadership function.

A. The Issue: *What is the core Issue in Collaborative Leadership?*

Lack of Collaborative Leadership is a core issue.
This can be revealed in several underlying challenges and signs.

B. The Signs: *What are the major Signs for lack of Collaborative Leadership?*

Here are some Signs that can be observed when there is lack of collaborative leadership in a governance system:
o Silo mentality and lack of coordination among the Agencies.
o Inadequate stakeholder engagement
o Unresponsive governance
o Lack of collective vision and goal-setting
o Disconnection between leaders and citizens

C. The Solutions: *Implications -What Solutions can help?*

Implement a Collaborative Leadership Approach to Governance.

The Purpose: The purpose for implementing a collaborative leadership approach to governance is to encourage and operate an inclusive strategy that involves cross-function stakeholders in the governance process.

Fostering collaborative leadership involves:
1. *Dialogue Across Party:* Encouraging politicians to engage in constructive dialogue across party lines.
2. *Building Coalitions:* Fostering partnerships among political parties, civil society, and stakeholders.
3. *Decision-Making Based on Consensus:* Encouraging politicians to prioritize national interests over party interests.
4. *Leadership Development Programs:* Training politicians in collaborative leadership skills.
5. *Collaboration Incentives:* Recognizing and rewarding politicians who demonstrate collaborative leadership.

Some Benefits of Collaborative Leadership

By fostering collaborative leadership, the government and society can:
1. Promote national unity.
2. Encourage bipartisan cooperation.
3. Address complex challenges through collective action.
4. Build trust among politicians and citizens.
5. Enhance innovation and governance effectiveness.
6. Promote more effective Communication among agencies.
7. Builder stronger relationships.
8. Improve decision-making.

Examples of Collaborative Leadership in Some Countries

Examples of collaborative leadership initiatives include the following:
1. The Germany's Grand Coalition: A coalition government of opposing parties working together.
2. The South Africa's Government of National Unity: A coalition government formed after apartheid.
3. The India's National Integration Council: A platform for politicians to discuss national issues.
4. The United States' Bipartisan Policy Center: A think tank promoting cross-party dialogue.
5. The Kenya's Building Bridges Initiative: A cross-party initiative to address national challenges.
In summary, a Collaborative Leadership approach can help address complex challenges of governance by encouraging politicians and leaders to prioritize national interests and work together towards common goals.

THIRTEEN

CONTINUOUS MONITORING AND EVALUATION

What is Continuous Monitoring and Evaluation?

I consider Continuous Monitoring and Evaluation [CM&E] as management functions for assessing the performance of a governance system [or any operation] and the progress of achievements of expected results. The purpose is to reveal gaps and issues in the system, to detect when and if the system is on-track or off-track, and apply corrective actions. In Project Management, they are often referred to as monitoring and control activities, and the control activity here emphasizes the corrective actions involved in the process. In some organizational setting, it can be referred to as Measurement and Evaluation [M&E] of results, making it more results and metrics focused. These functions help to ensure that resources are used effectively. Continuous Monitoring and Evaluation [CM&E] are crucial in good governance, ensuring accountability, transparency, and effectiveness.

A. The Issue: *What are the core Issues in Continuous Monitoring and Evaluation?*

Lack of Continuous Monitoring and Evaluation Processes in the Governance System is a core issue of governance.

The Issues of lack of Continuous Monitoring and Evaluation Processes in the governance system of a society cover the following areas:
o   Lack of clear objectives and indicators
o   Inadequate data collection and analysis
o   Ineffective feedback mechanisms
o   Political interference and bias
o   Inadequate reporting and dissemination
o   Limited stakeholder participation
o   Insufficient resources and capacity
o   Lack of follow-up and corrective action

B. The Signs: *What are the Signs of Lack of Continuous Monitoring and Evaluation in Governance?*

Here are some major Signs to watch out for to know when the governance system in a Society lacks continuous monitoring and evaluation:
o   Poor service delivery
o   Inadequate accountability
o   Lack of transparency
o   Inconsistent decision-making
o   Ineffective policy implementation

o Limited citizen engagement
o Inefficient use of resources
o High corruption levels

C. The Solutions: *The Implications - What Solutions can help?*

Provide, integrate and enforce Continuous Monitoring and Evaluation Processes in the governance system.

The Purpose: To assess the performance of the governance system and the progress of achievements of expected results, reveal gaps and issues in the system, to detect when the system is on-track or off-track and apply appropriate corrective actions, ensuring that the governance system is ruthlessly focused on the welfare and wellbeing of the citizens, the environment and the society in general.

Here are some Solutions to address the issues and signs of lack of continuous monitoring and evaluation processes in a governance system:
1. Establish clear objectives and indicators: It is on the basis of robustly established metrics of clear smart objectives [CSOs], key results areas [KRAs], and key performance indicators [KPIs], that performance can be focused, monitored, measured, assessed and evaluated effectively.

2. Invest in data collection and analysis capacity: Invest in capacity building and training.

3. Implement effective feedback mechanisms: Set up online and offline feedback Systems to monitor and evaluate public officers' services and performance. E.g. fill in Office, service obtained, name of officer, time attended to, any delays experienced, reason for delays, any gratifications requested, any other comments, etc.

4. Ensure independence and objectivity: Monitor the Monitor. Monitor Independent Oversight Institution as well.

5. Provide regular reporting and dissemination of feedbacks:

6. Ensure stakeholder participation and engagement:

7. Develop robust monitoring and evaluation frameworks: Build capacity and address systemic and structural issues; Embed and integrate CM&E in organizational culture.

8. Promote a culture of continuous learning and improvement: Use data-driven decision-making.

Some Benefits of CM&E in Good Governance

Some benefits of Continuous Monitoring and Evaluation Processes to a good governance system are listed here:

1. Improved accountability and transparency.
2. Enhanced effectiveness and efficiency.
3. Better decision-making.

4. Increased citizen trust and engagement.
5. Improved resource allocation.
6. Reduced corruption.
7. Enhanced learning and innovation.
8. Better policy implementation.

Some Tools and Techniques for C M & E

Here are some tools and techniques for monitoring, measuring and evaluating performance to foster a good governance system.

1. Citizen/Client Engagement Platforms: These digital platforms allow people to collaborate and participate in discussions and solutions, and contribute to the decision-making processes from anywhere. They can be used for Citizens'/Clients' Experiences and Feedback Platforms (online and offline), to report steadily on public services and performances, and to report on experience immediately after receiving public service from a public agency.

2. Road Maps and Logic Models: These are graphical illustrations or diagrams of how a program is expected to work, and they provide a clear and systemic way to identify and measure the inputs activities, outputs, and outcomes of a program. They are used to illustrate the relationship between a program's resources, the activities and the intended effects or impact or effects.

They are used to establish required input and activities for a program, in order to achieve desired output and outcome (results). They help to build a shared understanding and expectations among stakeholders and also enable identification of data for monitoring and improvement of the program.

3. *Theory of Change*: This is an explicit thought process for documenting how a program or intervention is supposed to work, stating the conditions for success and the benefits to all stakeholders, including the Society.

4. *Results Framework*: These are program-level frameworks for monitoring and evaluating program results and to adjust relevant activities as may be necessary. It focuses on how progress of achievements will be measured.

5. *Performance Indicators*: These are Key Performance Indicators (KPIs) for measuring performance over time for specific objectives. They provide target to focus on, milestones to assess progress and insights for better decisions.

6. *Data Analytics*: These processes allow organizations to obtain data and convert them into useful information for decision-making. Data Analytics helps organization to perform more efficiently and effectively by making more strategically-guided decisions.

7. *Social Audit:* This audit helps to measure, evaluate and report on social and ethical performance in a society and to access gaps between vision or goals and reality, and between efficiency and effectiveness.

8. *Public Expenditure Reviews [PERs]:* These are comprehensive assessments of government spending to ensure effectiveness, efficiency, and alignment with national priorities. They help to improve resource allocation and utilization, enhance transparency and accountability, and can strengthen public budget analysis and processes to better focus on growth and poverty reductions. Conducting regular PERs, helps governments to optimize their spending, achieve better outcomes, and ensure fiscal sustainability.

By implementing continuous monitoring and evaluation, governments and organizations can ensure accountability, transparency, and effectiveness, ultimately leading to better governance and improved outcomes.

Examples of Some Countries and Organizations That Apply CM&E

Here are some examples of some Countries and Organizations that implement continuous monitoring and evaluation processes in their Governance System:

1. Australia's Performance Management and Evaluation Framework.
2. Canada's Treasury Board Secretariat's Evaluation Policy.
3. United Kingdom's National Audit Office.
4. World Bank's Results-Based Monitoring and Evaluation.
5. United Nations Development Program's (UNDP) Monitoring and Evaluation Framework.
6. European Commission's Monitoring and Evaluation Framework.

FOURTEEN

FINAL THOUGHTS

I have listed here my final thoughts about bad governance and good governance and to focus attention and our mindset to move from the bad to the good.

What Bad Governance May Mean to the Citizens

Bad Governance is the absence or lack of Good Governance. Bad Governance may mean so many improprieties in the governance system of a society, such as the following and more:

1. Lack of effective leadership and management of national resources.

2. Lack of transparency and accountability of leaders and the government

3. Lack of care for the citizens' welfare and security

4. Lack of care for environmental welfare and security

5. Lack of freedom of speech, movement and residence

6. Lack of adequate food security for the Citizens
7. Lack of adequate shelter for the Citizens
8. Lack of basic Infrastructure in the Society
9. Lack of Citizens Participation
10. Abuse and misuse of political power by Leaders/Government
11. Abuse and misuse law enforcement agencies powers
12. Ineffective Rule of Law – where some Leaders and politicians live above the law.
13. Extravagant lifestyle of political leaders and the government – condoning irresponsible and reckless behaviour in office and public life.
14. Creating an atmosphere of discord and fear.
15. Lack of economic development.
16. Economic crisis and collapse.
17. Illicit enrichment of public officers
18. Leadership extravagance and recklessness
19. Irresponsive Leader
20. Promoting selfish monopolies for essential products and commodities, products and services
21. Promoting vicious ethnic division
22. The mass citizenry do not benefit from national wealth and resources

23. Only a few sacred cows are benefiting from the national wealth and resources.

24. Drastic and hasty reforms of any sort and kind. For example, energy reform involving immediate conversion from premium motor spirit [PMS] fuel to compressed natural gas [CNG] fuel for automobile vehicles; financial reform involving a change from controlled foreign exchange rate to free market-driven foreign exchange rate in a mainly consumption non-production import-dependent economy. Such drastic reforms can adversely implicate national economy and citizens' welfare and living standards.

25. Lack of development in the society.

What Good Governance May Mean to the Citizens

Good Governance on the other hand is what leaders and citizens should focus on. It is the hope of all citizens, though it may be elusive in several society especially Africa. Citizens expect good government to mean the following listed actions and experiences and more:

1. Empowerment of the Citizens – provision enabling environment and infrastructures for responsible citizens' livelihoods.
2. Welfare and wellbeing of the Citizens – food security and provision of free Medicare for the children and senior citizens of the society.
3. Security of the Citizens – freedom to move around, live around, stay alive and speak up in Society without illegitimate molestations.
4. Food security for the Citizens.
5. Shelter for the Citizens.
6. Affordable healthcare for all.
7. Free and Fair electoral processes.
8. Fostering physical democratic dividends.
9. Environmental protection and security.
10. Transparency and accountability of public officers.
11. Citizens' participation in affairs that affect their wellbeing and their Nation.
12. Citizens' freedom to thrive and prosper.
13. Fostering an egalitarian society
14. Building a Nation of Laws, not of men
15. Effective Rule of Law
16. Freedom of speech
17. Citizens' Education and Awareness – free and compulsory for all children

18. Gradual Reforms of all kinds
19. Good governance should target valuing lives and the natural environment – the live of every individual in particular, the habitat environment and the society in general
20. Immediate consequences and punishment for crime of public officers and officials holding offices in public trust.
21. Power to the people
22. Merit-based appointments
23. Citizens' access to information
24. Continuous improvement in development of the society
25. A truly representative system of government.

What Are Your Thoughts?

This is an opportunity for you to articulate and list your views and thoughts about what Bad Governance and Good Governance may mean to you in your clime, country or in any part of the world. Thank you!

A. What does Bad Governance mean to you?

1.

2.

3.

4.

5

6.

7.

8.

9.

10.

B. What does Good Governance Mean To You?

1.

2.

3.

4.

5

6.

7.

8.

9.

10.

AFTERWORD

BRILLIANT Implementations of the recommended governance solutions [nuggets, guides and templates] can be the key to good governance in a society that yearns to become egalitarian and prosperous. Some or all of these nuggets, guides and templates may already be on paper and existing in some or most African societies, but implementations may not have been at their best for the common good of the citizens. The implementations require more than focus, but ruthless focus and rigor.

Examples abound. Some Federations are not truly federated, but suffering from lack of decentralization and devolution of powers. In some other societies, the anti-corruption agencies can hardly book or prosecute some sacred cows; even at the fringe of serious crimes, they may turn away their faces from crimes of party members. The agencies are supposed to be independent and above politics.

Therefore, a ruthless focus on the brilliant implementation of the solutions can seal the open doors of bad governance, and open the closed doors for good governance to thrive. I have made some summary notes here of the solutions proffered in this book.

Chapter Summary Notes of the Solutions

To address the complex challenges [Issues and Signs] that affect good governance in a society, the following simple good governance solutions should be considered:

1. Effective Leadership and Management: Set and communicate a clear vision, smart goals and objectives for citizens' and environment's well-being, welfare and security.

2. Transparency and Accountability: Implement open governance systems, ensuring citizens can access information and track government activities.

3. Decentralization and Devolution: Empower local governments to make decisions and manage resources, promoting fiscal federalism.

4. Independent Institutions: Strengthen independent bodies like anti-corruption agencies, electoral commissions, and judiciaries.

5. Citizen Participation: Encourage citizen engagement in decision-making processes through town hall meetings, public consultations, and inclusive policy-making.

6. Merit-Based Appointments: Replace federal quota systems with merit-based appointments to ensure competence and reduce nepotism.

7. Asset Declaration: Mandate asset declaration for politicians and public officials to combat corruption.

8. Simplified and Digitalized Processes: Streamline government processes, reducing bureaucracy and opportunities for corruption.

9. Education and Awareness: Promote civic education, emphasizing the importance of good governance, transparency, and accountability.

10. Effective Rule of Law: Implement and enforce effective Rule of Law, by providing a framework that ensures that power is exercised in a fair, accountable, and transparent manner, promoting justice, stability, and prosperity.

11. Gradual Reforms: Implement gradual, incremental reforms, allowing for adaptation and minimizing resistance.

12. Collaborative Leadership: Foster a culture of collaborative leadership, encouraging politicians to work together for the nation's benefit.

13. Continuous Monitoring and Evaluation: Provide, integrate and enforce Continuous Monitoring and Evaluation Processes in the governance system.

14. Final Thoughts: This is an opportunity to articulate some list of thoughts to focus on as what good governance may mean to a citizen of any nation. Note the list is not exhaustive. Remember, effective and good governance requires patience, persistence, and collective effort from citizens, leaders, and institutions.

ACKNOWLEDMENT

MY special thanks and appreciation go to God Almighty for the inspiration and enablement to put my inspired thoughts into written words for the benefits of mankind at this appropriate timing when most societies are fraught with the dire and urgent need for good governance.

My next level of inspiration came from the people of my Country Nigeria, that were driven by earnest concern and passion for the Country to the extent of pouring out, their overflowing emotions against bad governance, into the streets of various cities in the Country. This also fired illumination into my putting these thoughts on good governance together. I very much appreciate them all, and everyone with the enthusiasm and zeal to make Nigeria, Africa and the World a better place to live in.

I also appreciate all my family members, friends and mentors who have in various ways contributed to my thoughts and resources expressed in this book. I thank you all!

ABOUT THE AUTHOR

Jonathan Oyibo PMP, the author of this book, is blessed with a very robust career experience in commercial projects management. He served in various functional and leadership capacities and has built capabilities in that field for over thirty five years in the past, and as a continuing Consultant till date. He is a certified Project Management Professional in good standing. He is now also engaged in writing and coaching, with a strong passion for people development.
Email: oyibo.jonathan@yahoo.co.uk

Other Books By The Author

1. **Life of a Brand:** Seven Stages from Embryo to Transition.
2. **7Fs of Risk Management:** A Friendly Approach.
3. **Tales from the Scriptures:** Blessing Stories.
4. **Tales from the Scriptures:** Mystery and Miracle Stories.

Notes:

Notes

www.ingramcontent.com/pod-product-compliance
Lightning Source LLC
Chambersburg PA
CBHW061356250726
48657CB00004B/1516